All You Need to Find Success Is Here

All You Need to Find Success Is Here

Nelson Navas Ortega

iUniverse, Inc.
New York   Bloomington

iUniverse books may be ordered through booksellers or by contacting:

iUniverse
1663 Liberty Drive
Bloomington, IN 47403
www.iuniverse.com
1-800-Authors (1-800-288-4677)

Because of the dynamic nature of the Internet, any Web addresses or links contained in this book may have changed since publication and may no longer be valid. The views expressed in this work are solely those of the author and do not necessarily reflect the views of the publisher, and the publisher hereby disclaims any responsibility for them.

ISBN: 978-1-4401-7966-2 (sc)
ISBN: 978-1-4401-7384-4 (ebook)

Printed in the United States of America

iUniverse rev. date: 10/14/09

For Jackelin, Miguel, and Marianna.
For those out there who inspired me.

Prologue

A few years ago my life changed. It was a profound change that made me reevaluate my life. I reconsidered all I had done until that point and thought about where I was going. I found that I had moderate success in my career. I had overcome many financial hurdles, and things seemed to be more stable. I had reached a point where I could say that I had some level of success—my situation had improved over time.

However, when I began to consider the future, things didn't seem so clear. I had no goals. I had a nice job but was not really enjoying it. I had to face the fact that I had settled. I was doing the bare minimum to survive, but I was not really living. I didn't know where I was going. I had no direction and nothing to look forward to. This is a very dangerous place to be. Does this sound familiar?

The time had come to make a decision. Soon I would be learning that this was the first basic step toward finding a direction in life. The alternatives were clear and simple: do nothing or do something. The decision, however, was not an easy one. Doing nothing was easier and, in fact, that is what I had been doing for a long time. I knew that doing something was the right alternative, but it was a hard one to choose.

What was I going to do? What was that something that needed to be done?

I had read somewhere that you're supposed to have goals in life. I didn't have any, so I started to create a lot of them. I wrote the goals down, as the experts recommended, but this did not help me. My goals were all oriented toward one thing: money. After all, successful people have a lot of money and live the life of their dreams, right? There was nothing wrong with my goals, but the problem was that I hadn't thought about what I wanted to do to earn this money.

By the time I finished high school, the only way I knew to make a living was to be an engineer. Being a medical doctor was the other alternative, but that never interested me a lot. So I got into an university and started to study electronics engineering. I failed miserably in college. By the end of my first college year I had failed most of the subjects, and I was kicked out of that university.

I was told by my family that I had to enroll in another college. I remembered that the only subject I ever passed was computer programming. I enrolled in a new college in computer science. There I was lucky to find something I enjoyed. I found that with little effort I could get a lot of things accomplished. In most of the subjects that a lot of people were having problems with, I was excelling and having the time of my life. When complicated problems were given to me, I actually looked forward to resolving them. I spent long hours learning and playing with computers, but it never felt like a chore. I never felt like I was doing some superhuman effort, and I did not need any will to get me to do my work. I learned how easy it is to find success if you really love what you do.

I had the material success. I was not a millionaire but for the things I liked to do I had plenty. However, there was something missing and I could not figure out what it was. I needed to find out.

This was not an easy thing to do. Imagine spending fifteen years in a career and discovering that what once gave you a lot of satisfaction was simply an empty routine. I had spent my entire professional life focusing on only one thing; I didn't know anything else. Nothing was clear to me anymore. My life, supposedly stable, was not going anywhere. Indeed, I was lost.

It is only when you realize how lost you are that you can be found. I started looking everywhere. I read books. I searched the Internet. I was looking for something, but didn't know what it was. One day, during one of my Internet searches, I found some text about how our world had been created and how it has evolved over time. I thought it was just science fiction but it was very interesting, so I read the whole thing. In those pages I came across a word that sounded familiar: Urantia. I had heard that word before, but I couldn't remember where.

The text I was reading was a part of the Urantia book. This book is not a sacred book and it is not the new Bible. It is not the manifesto of a new religion either. It is just a good source of information. I read the entire book, and I was inspired. After I read the book, I was struck by one idea in particular: that there is a God and He is inside each one of us.

I started to repeat that idea in my head. After some time, like a dumb, lost idiot, I ventured to infer that if God was inside each one of us, could it be that … maybe … He was inside me too? How slow we are to grasp new ideas. A lot of things did not make sense. There was a God and He was one person, however, He was also inside each one of us. Perhaps He was even inside me. How was this possible? There were a lot of contradictions; it was too fantastic to believe, too good to be true. And yet, I couldn't get rid of the idea that He, the celestial Father Himself, was so close to me.

Time passed by and I wanted to learn more and more. One day I decided that I would believe that God was inside of me, and things started to happen. I found myself talking with the Father and getting some answers. Some things that were so difficult before started to become clearer, and my life began to have a meaning. I discovered that religion is not what we think it is. It's just a personal relationship with God.

You may ask, what does this have to do with success? When you realize that the source of all inspiration resides within you, perceived limitations vanish. You come to realize that you have a purpose. You didn't just appear in the world one day. You are here for some reason, and if you find that reason, you will find success.

This book will give you the knowledge to be the best you can be. This is not a book about religion, but God is in this book. Actually, there is not a place where He is not. In this book you will learn what you need to do to reach your potential. You will get the facts in the clearest and simplest way possible. I can only speak from my personal experience, but I want you to know that I am not special. I am not smarter than anyone else. I didn't have better opportunities than anyone else. I was not born rich, but I did not come from misery either. I'm just a regular guy. So if I found success, there's absolutely no reason why you can't find it too. I was looking out there for success and satisfaction. It was only when I started looking within me that everything started to happen. The inspiration and orientation for the life you want to live lies inside you, just waiting to be discovered.

This book is about success, but it is also an invitation for you to start a lifetime exploration, a journey of self-discovery. You need to know yourself on the inside before attempting to produce something on the outside. Before starting to read this book, I want you to consider the idea that changed my life and I invite you to make the same inference on your own as well. "If God is inside each one of us, and the author says that he realized that He was inside him as well, could it be that ... maybe ... He's inside me too?"

Before You Begin

The level of satisfaction you're experiencing in your life is a direct result of the depth of your relationship with the divine in yourself. The presence of the Father within you is what provides that sense of accomplishment.

You can be very successful in the eyes of others. It may look like you have everything you need to be successful. However, what you feel inside yourself has no relation to what others think of you. If your material needs are fulfilled but your needs as a spiritual being are not met, you will always feel that something is missing. People who achieve this kind of success, external success, do not find satisfaction, and they fall into the trap of accumulation. Nothing seems to fill them, so they start buying more things, more entertainment, more pleasures, and still they feel empty. This is not the kind success you will attain using the principles of this book.

Real success is something that can be felt without a doubt. When real success is part of your life *you will know* you are successful. After understanding and applying the four principles of this book, you will know you are being successful, regardless of external appearances.

You will have mastered the idea of success. Success will not be a destination. You will be thinking, working, playing, and having fun in a successful state of mind. You will not have to wait years to experience success. You will not have to check the balance of your bank account to confirm your success. You will know without hesitation that you are a successful person. This will come from your newfound way of looking at your life, work, and relationships. This is the success mentality.

One of the things you have to consider is that success is a process, not a result. Therefore, your idea of success should be independent of the results you expect to obtain. Success is a way of life. It is a positive and optimistic way to look at everything that arises in your daily life. When you focus only on results, any surprises you encounter along the way are considered problems because they may not seem to contribute to what you expect. When you live successfully, every surprise is an opportunity. Living successfully means not having expectations about the future. When you have the success mentality you *know* that any new situation is always an opportunity to explore, learn, and grow.

Having the success mentality will change your perception on your life. You will notice that you seem to be taking advantage of every new opportunity that comes to you. You will feel like you are attracting opportunities because they come more often than you've experienced before. This is what some call the law of attraction—a tendency to attract the good things that help you to move forward. The reality is that when you have a restricted state of mind and your thoughts are not really under control, your mind can't perceive anything new. It's not that you are not receiving enough opportunities. What is actually happening is that you are not paying attention. Every conversation is an opportunity; every new person you meet is an opportunity; every book you read is an opportunity. Opportunities are abundant. Each person in this world is an opportunity. You will never be in a place where there are no opportunities available to you. You just need to open your eyes and expand your mind.

The problem with opportunities is that we like to classify them. We like to control what happens around us. When you think about the opportunities you like to have, you always attach very definite qualities to them. I wish "this" would happen to me. When you consider what "this" is, you also usually have a very specific idea about how you want "this" to be. The problem is that what you want does not always come the way you want it.

One of the things I always thought would be nice was to be interviewed on a radio show. It would be a great opportunity to express some of my ideas to a larger audience and to see how I would like it. I used to think it would be great if someone invited me to do a radio interview. However, I never got an invitation. Instead, someone asked me to be in charge of the registration process for a conference. That was going to be a lot of work and I was already busy. But I thought maybe something positive would come out of it and I might even learn some new skills so, why not? A couple of weeks later, the person in charge of the conference was invited to a radio station to promote the conference and she invited me too, because I was in charge of registration. So I was able to be on the radio, but it didn't happen the way I expected. If I had decided to save myself several late nights of work, I would have missed the chance to do what I wanted to do. This is where exploration and the success mentality will pay off. Every unexpected event in your life is an opportunity since you don't really know what good things may come from it.

In a more spiritual sense, this way of looking at life is called faith. True faith is living with the awareness that God exerts control over everything. On top of that, He loves us. Therefore, everything in the universe is created so we can make our dreams come true. But the only way to do this is to go with the flow, to swim with the current, not against it. This means dedicating your life to the Father's will. His will is best for us. It makes us happier and allows us to grow.

When you think that you know what is best for you, you start coming up with your own wants and needs. These are usually things that will not provide the satisfaction you expect, even if you manage to achieve them. You start focusing your energy and your efforts on making those things happen. Then it all starts to feel hard, difficult. You will start trying to reorganize the universe, the people around you, and your life, to serve your own purposes. This is a lot of work for a single human being. When you do this, you are swimming upstream. You are struggling, and you are not accomplishing anything worthwhile.

When you learn to trust, you first learn to let go. You immediately feel as if a load has been taken off your shoulders. You start experiencing this new state of being, and as your mind relaxes and your feelings calm, you start seeing all those opportunities that used to go unnoticed before. By living this way, your fears will vanish. You'll realize that there's nothing to fear. Your life, your destiny, and your future are in perfect hands, literally. You just need to open yourself to the possibilities and start exploring everything that He has set in your path. This is true religion. It is just getting to know that light within you—getting to know your Father.

To be successful, you will need to lead a religious life. Some people get really scared when they hear this for the first time. I do not mean religion in the way we usually encounter it. A good way to clarify religion and establish its real meaning is to decide what religion is not. Religion is not going to church frequently. Religion is not even belonging to a church. Religion is not being good. Religion is not repeating memorized prayers over and over again. Religion has nothing to do with the way you dress or the way you decorate your body. Religion has nothing to do with defending your home, your city, or your country. Religion is not your way of life. Religion is not trying to convince others of what you believe. Religion is not reading a book. Religion is not a matter of groups or organizations. Religion is not morality. Religion is not rules. Religion is not sacrifice.

If we take all these things away from religion, what's left? Religion is just finding God inside you and establishing a relationship with Him. Religion is just each person's quest to meet his or her creator. Religion is love and freedom. That's all. You don't need temples or rituals. You don't need to tell anybody. It's just something between you and God. Can you feel this truth in your heart? Can you see that you have known this all along? The great truths are always inside us, since the Father is in each one of us. Sometimes we just need to see them or hear them to realize that we already knew them. You can start living a religious life today, right now. Ask yourself what is inside you. Ask the Father to be present right here with you. He already is here with you, but this exercise will open your mind to this possibility and will make you more receptive. Do this often. Just talk to the Father and feel His answers. Better yet, write His answers down. You will discover Him inside you and you will have access to a very powerful resource in your life, one that will help you grow and progress.

1

Decide

Our current jobs, the places we live, our friends, our lives—everything is a consequence of our decisions. We are where we are because of the decisions we have made in the past. If you are in a job you don't like, it's because you put yourself in that situation. You decided to apply for that job. You decided to accept that job when it was offered to you, and when you realized that you didn't like that job, you decided to stay in it. Your decisions determine the life you live.

This seems self-evident, right? The example above can be applied to any area of your life. But from that obvious statement you can deduce the following: if my life today is a consequence of yesterday's decisions, then my life tomorrow will be a consequence of today's decisions. In other words, today you are creating your future. This is powerful. This means that the decisions you make today create the type of life you will be living tomorrow.

If you want things to change, if you want to have a different life, a better life, then your decisions have to change. Your style of decision making in the past has brought you to where you are now. If you keep doing the same thing, you will get the same results, the same future.

Therefore, here is the first decision you need to make: Do you really want to change?

Before you make a decision, I invite you consider the following: How can you tell if something is alive? What is one definite characteristic shared by all living things? This is the mother of all oxymorons, but the only constant thing in our world is change. All living beings are constantly changing. They are moving from one state to the next. Movement is the one common attribute that is shared by all living things. Even plants move. Every day plants grow, their cells expand, and they take energy and transform it. Life in our world, and in the entire universe, is always changing, evolving, advancing. Those who cease to move are not living anymore.

For human beings this is more relevant. We are spiritual beings; there is more to us than just flesh and bone. Even when our bodies reach maturity, our minds and our spirits continue to progress and grow. So before you decide that you want to stay just where you are, ask yourself: Do you think you've reached your highest potential? Do you think there's nothing else to discover and achieve? I will give you a hint: no one in this world has reached his or her highest potential. And no one will because there is not a moment during our spiritual growth where we could say that there is nothing else to learn.

The right decision is to change, to progress, to keep moving, to live. Whether you are doing what you absolutely love or you are lost trying to find your way, there is always room for improvement. Time is your most valuable possession. You should not waste it doing things that will not help you improve. You have the divine right to do whatever you want to do. You have the right to live the life you want to live. But you have to decide to go for it. It is always up to you.

With each new decision comes uncertainty. These are the "what ifs." You ask yourself, "Am I doing the right thing?" How could you be certain that you are doing the right thing, making the right decision? There is always a way to determine if you are making the right decision. Here is where that Father's presence within you will help. The best course of action is to follow the will of your Father in heaven. This is what confuses most people. I need to follow the Father's will, but I also need to make my own decisions? How does this work?

You have been created for a purpose. You have potential in you that no other person has. Your personality is unique and is perfect for your particular purpose in life. When you discover the things in which you can be the best you can be, you are following the Father's design for you. Those are also the things from which you will get the most satisfaction. Those are the things in which you will find success beyond your dreams. But you always have the final word. You have to decide to try those things.

Following the Father's will is deciding to take the opportunities He presents to us. You will find that when you start exploring and looking for something, new opportunities will present themselves, apparently out of nowhere, and you are the one who must decide to take them or not. When you face a decision you can feel whether the decision is right or wrong. Your emotions can confirm that you are making the right decision, and with this confirmation you can be confident that the outcome of that decision will be good for you and others.

The internal presence of the Father confirms or denies our thoughts and decisions through our emotions. This is what some call intuition. You have felt it before. Sometimes you face a new situation and somehow you know, you feel, that it's going to be good or bad for you.

Learning to trust in your emotions is a gradual process. You may not recognize the emotions associated with a decision you make today. Before you can do that, there is one thing that you must understand and accept. Some ideas will be inspired by the Father's presence in you. You need to identify whether an idea comes from the Father or from your own imagination. To determine whether an idea or an emotion comes from the Father, you must consider three characteristics: truth, beauty, and goodness. If the idea or emotion does not satisfy these three elements, then it was not inspired by the Father. This is how you can separate your own emotions and ideas from the ones that are inspired by the Father.

The same criteria apply to opportunities. If a new opportunity you encounter does not satisfy the criteria of truth, beauty, and goodness, then you can safely say no to it and move on. You will not lose anything valuable by rejecting those things that will not help you to be successful. In fact, you will be saving a lot of time and energy that would have been wasted.

Most importantly, if the emotion associated with a decision does not satisfy the criteria of truth, beauty, and goodness, you have to seriously consider the reason you are feeling that particular emotion. This is so important, because there is one emotion that is always present in us and does not meet our criteria: fear.

Fear is our darkest and most dangerous emotion. Fear is not an emotion inspired by the Father's presence. However, this is the emotion that influences our decisions most of the time. Whenever you are making a decision and the only emotion that prevents you from acting is fear, then you have no valid reason to avoid making that decision. Fear should never be what stops you from moving forward.

Let me clarify a little more. Let's say that you are about to make a decision about something. You know that if you make that decision your actions and the possible outcome of that decision will be an expression of truth, beauty, and goodness. It will be an expression of love. However, you start coming up with excuses. You start creating reasons why you should not do it. You start imagining what would happen if you fail. This is fear. Do not be influenced by fear. Do not let fear get in the way of your dreams, of the life you want to live.

The process of making good decisions is this: evaluate the emotions associated with the decision; apply the truth, beauty, and goodness criteria; and make sure that the only thing preventing you from making that decision is not fear. This process is simple enough, but it will require practice, discipline, and most of all, courage. But this is the first step on your ladder to success. Without this nothing else will work.

Having the ability to make the right decisions will help you create the life and the future you were meant to have. Our Father in heaven did not create us to suffer. He is a loving Father, better than we can imagine, and He wants the best for us. Being successful is our intended destination, but some of us get lost along the way. This happens because we could not follow directions, our Father's directions. Now you know what to do to make sure you are going the right way.

2

Be The Master Of Yourself

How great could you be if you had absolute control of your mind? What if, after you have made a decision, you could be sure that you will do all it takes to achieve the desired result? You would become unstoppable and failure would be impossible. In order to take this control, you need to master yourself.

How many times have you failed at something without knowing why? Maybe you have various excuses: the time wasn't right, it was too hard, it was not for me, it was somebody else's fault, and so on. But can you really say that you gave all you had to give? Or was someone sabotaging your efforts?

Typically the latter is true. Someone is sabotaging you. Someone is doing things that take you further away from your goal. For each thing you did right, that person did two things wrong. You know who that person is. Right now that person is trying to remain hidden and is afraid of being recognized. But you know who that person is and you will not blame that person because that person is someone very close and very dear to you. But this is the time you decided to take control of your life and that person needs to play accordingly, so accept this fact: that person is you.

This happens so often that it's almost a miracle that we have any self-esteem left. One of the most common goals people have is to lose weight. We live in a world where we have a current epidemic of obesity and we are also obsessed by the distorted images of beauty with which the media regularly bombards us. We all know that the best way to fight obesity is by eating better and exercising more. Many start doing this and the majority fails. They fail not because the goal is unworthy but because they decide that they can't do it. They don't have enough control over their minds and bodies to establish a reasonable level of discipline. And be aware that when I say "they," I am including you and me. It's easier to say that "they" have a problem instead of "we" have a problem.

Once we have made a decision, we need to have the discipline to do what is required to achieve the expected result. Deciding to change will not do us any good without the will to change. When making a decision, think of it as standing at a crossroad, deciding which direction to take. Once you know where you're going, you'll need to start walking and keep walking in order to find your destination. It's not enough to know where you are going—you have to walk there.

You have to be able to make yourself do what you need to do. You have to be able to control your inner resources, your intelligence, your ideas, and your body in order to achieve your full potential. At the end of your life, only you can explain why you did or did not achieve your dreams. Now is the time to be honest with yourself and find out what you need to change. This may be painful for some and quite uncomfortable, but it is an effort that will pay off handsomely.

As humans, we exist in three different levels: soul, mind, and body. We need to take this order into account when making adjustments. This is what we need to consider when selecting the behaviors that will help us on our way, while replacing the bad habits that hinder our progress and determine our lack of success.

Your soul contains your highest and purest aspirations. This is the part of you that really does not need anything but to be identified with its source. This is the part that yearns for the spirit within you, the presence of the Father—your guiding light. The only sustenance this part of you needs is to become more and more in touch with God. This level of existence does not get involved with life in the material world, but it's the part of us we need to care for the most because it is our true self.

At the soul level there is only one emotion: Love. Notice that I used uppercase L because it's not just love as we usually perceive it. This Love is not possessiveness, friendship, or affection. The Love at this level is pure energy. In fact, it is the energy that sustains the universe and all life. It is very hard to describe because it is something we need to keep exploring and experimenting with in order to understand it. For example, a child experiences Love for his or her parents and siblings. When the child grows, he or she finds that special someone and they achieve a deeper understanding of Love. Later, that child, now an adult, will have children too, and this will bring an additional depth to the concept of Love. If that person is lucky enough to establish a relation with the Father and experience unconditional Love, the concept of Love takes on another dimension. Consequently, as the person progresses, Love becomes more present, more ubiquitous, and its effects over everything about him or her becomes more apparent. Our understanding of Love will deepen as we progress and obtain wisdom. Love is the only feeling that stimulates our soul. All the other feelings belong to the mind.

The only thing we can do within our soul is to explore our relationship with the Father. This is the main purpose of human existence, and when this search is honest and consistent, we feel the benefits in our minds and bodies. Do not dismiss this part of your life because if you do you will perceive that happiness seems to elude you, and no level of success will ever satisfy you completely. If you want to experience success at its fullest, you need to be at peace in your soul. I will go as far as to say that if you search for the Father within your soul, then nothing else will matter.

Next is the mind. This is where our material life is constructed. This is where we take the input from the spirit within us and make it into something concrete and applicable. This is the part of yourself that you need to control and make sure you use it to its fullest. You must learn to control your mind. Before learning what you need to do to make your mind work for you, there is something you have to understand about the nature of the mind. If I ask you to point to your brain, you will know exactly where to point your finger. We know that the brain is inside our heads. However, there is not a definitive location for the mind. It is not a bodily organ. We cannot really point to a place and say, "Here is our mind." The mind is not a part of our body.

The mind is what we use to express ourselves in the world. Even though it is not a part of our body, it clearly is a part of us. Through our mind we experience the world, we obtain and create knowledge, and, with a little spiritual connection, we develop wisdom. All of us understand this in one form or another. However, there is one characteristic of the mind we tend to overlook sometimes. Think about this: How many minds exist in our world today? Doesn't each person in the world have a mind? Actually, there is only one mind.

We are like fish in the ocean. The mind is the ocean and each one of us uses it individually and shapes it into whatever we want. We like to claim a portion for ourselves, but this does not change the fact that it is a shared resource. The implications of this are astounding. The way we think and our ideas are not just ours alone. One person may have an original idea somewhere in the world and another person may get a similar idea in a different part of the world, without any contact between the two.

This happens so often that science historians have a name for this phenomenon: "multiples." Many inventions were invented almost simultaneously, in different parts of the world. William Ogburn and Dorothy Thomas, in 1922, put together a list of "multiples" in which they found that 148 inventions or discoveries were made simultaneously in different parts of the world. Some of the discoveries include calculus, decimal fractions, oxygen, and sunspots. Some of the inventions include the telephone, color photography, and the telescope.[1]

In nature it is more evident that there is only one mind. Studying flocks of birds or schools of fishes, we can see how all individuals seem to move together like one unit, as if they were part of a single organism. Animals are just a little more in sync with using the shared resource that is the mind. It is the same mind we use—we just use a little more of it.

There are two major implications of realizing that there is only one mind and that it is a shared resource. First, you are influenced by the thinking of the people around you. It's widely accepted that the offspring of successful people often become successful. This is because the children of successful people grow up believing that the possibility of achieving success is very real, and not a remote or vain hope. Similarly, the children of unsuccessful people, troubled families, people with issues, often inherit the same thought patterns and will most likely end up living similar lives.

The second implication is more positive and empowering: you can influence people with the way you think. By having a positive attitude, you can have a positive influence on those around you. A positive attitude goes a long way. Encouragingly, it's easy to replace negative ways of thinking with positive thoughts because people tend to repeat the behaviors that make them feel good. It is common sense—when something is good we want more of it. If something feels bad, painful, or stressful, we don't want anymore of that.

This is good news and the key to changing our behaviors. We know that we have some bad habits. We know that we would be better off without them. We have all tried to change many times with various degrees of success. But the changes have never been deep enough or lasting. The problem is that our approach to attacking this problem is flawed. We tend to take a bad habit and just try hard to stop doing it. We muster all of our will to *not* do something. This creates a sense of deprivation in our mind. We did whatever the wrong behavior was because we enjoyed it. So we are actually removing something that

1   Malcolm Gladwell, *Annals of Innovation: In the Air. The New Yorker*, May 12, 2008.

provided pleasure and are creating a void in our lives. Naturally, this type of change is not sustainable. Sooner or later we will have to fill that void again and we will inevitably revert to those old behaviors because that's the only way we can fill that void.

There is another way to kick out those bad habits for good. Whenever you need to get rid of a negative behavior, replace it with something positive. This way there will be no void in your life. Instead of doing something that is not good for you, you'll be doing something positive that makes you feel good. This way you are reinforcing the good behavior because you are feeling good each time you do it. This is a more natural way to address bad habits. You will not be creating a void. You will be doing something good instead.

For example, let's say you have a habit of watching TV for six hours a day (this is actually the American average). Every day you realize you have lost six hours of your life in which you didn't do anything useful. You know you have to change. If you decide just to turn off the TV and do nothing else, you will be creating a void. You will feel like the time passes slowly. The six hours will feel like twelve because you haven't filled your time with something else. Using the positive approach, you can fill the time with positive activities, such as reading, exercising, or talking with friends. The key is that it must be something that makes you feel good. If you decide to read a book, read something that interests you. If you just read something you don't enjoy, you'll get bored very quickly and revert to watching TV again. If you read a book that you enjoy, you will be more likely to keep doing it. If you decide to exercise, you will notice the benefits almost immediately and you'll want to exercise even more. Be creative and start replacing those habits you don't need with the behaviors that will make you progress in the right direction. If you do it this way, you are removing the difficult part out of the process—your own resistance.

Next, you need to learn to control your thoughts. Our mind is usually filled with constant chatter. During one of your routine activities, pause for a moment. You'll notice how we seem to be bombarded by all sorts of thoughts. The mind is always busy processing more information than it can handle efficiently. This doesn't have to be the case.

Many of these thoughts are not productive. These thoughts do not accomplish anything useful in our lives. The most common thoughts of this kind are worries and concerns. These are negative thoughts because they keep us distracted and unable to process additional input. Many of us complain that we don't get enough opportunities to succeed, but what actually happens is that our mind is so busy that it can't accept anything different than our normal thought patterns. Opportunities fall into this category because they are always surprises. Opportunities are situations that fall outside our normal parameters—the comfort zone. In order to explore these opportunities, we must venture into unknown terrain. Opportunities provide us with a chance to grow, to progress, and to expand our mind. People who are successful are known for finding opportunities where nobody else sees them. This is not luck—it's just that their mind is more open and receptive.

You can train your mind to function like this. The idea is to get rid of all the thoughts that are not helping you, such as worries, anxieties, or concerns. These thoughts are based on the premise that something bad may happen. They are a big waste of time and mental energy. What is the purpose of wasting our energy thinking about something that *may* happen? If something bad is going to happen, you won't be able to mitigate the damage by thinking about it before it happens. You would actually be doubling your suffering because you would have been thinking about it while everything was still fine. However, more often than not, the bad things you dread never happen.

In addition to eliminating worries and concerns, you must monitor self-sabotaging thoughts. These thoughts limit you. Each time you say "I can't," "I'm unable," "I'm incapable," you are creating a sense of inadequacy. These thoughts impose false limits on what you think you can achieve because you can only do what you believe you can do.

These false limits control you behavior. Each time you say you can't do something, you won't. This is not because of some magical influence that negative thoughts have over your reality; it's because you can only do what you tell yourself you can do. Think about it. If you have the idea that you can't do something, the first time you try to do it and fail, your mind will tell you, "Of course. I told you that you can't do it." Then you just quit. Now if you tell yourself that you *can* do it, things are different. You may still fail the first time you try something new. However, your mind tells you, "You can do it." You try a different approach and you fail again. Your mind keeps telling you, "You can do it." Hence, you will keep trying until you achieve your goal because you expect yourself to succeed. Can you see how something as simple as positive thinking can have an influence on your life and your success?

You must also strive to remove hateful thoughts from your mind. Hateful thoughts are very negative because they are the opposite of Love. This type of thinking has a definite adverse influence over our well-being, which includes both our mental and physical health. As mentioned before, Love is the energy that sustains the universe. When we allow the opposite of Love in our lives, we are just poisoning ourselves.

To rid ourselves of hateful thoughts, we can use forgiveness. Hate is usually a defense mechanism that we adopt when somebody or something hurt us. Hate is a strong emotion that can cloud everything else, which makes it useful as a shield. If something hurt us, we use hate to numb our feelings. However, we pay a very high price for this protection. Hate will block our natural ability to relate to our brothers and sisters in the world. Hate also spawns many other feelings that contribute to our isolation: distrust, envy, and revenge. We were created to work together. Isolation makes our personalities wither and our creativity diminish. Clearly, if you want to achieve true success in your life, hate is something that should never enter your mind.

You must learn to forgive all the people who have caused you pain in your life, including yourself. Revisiting these painful episodes at first may seem like an act of masochism. However, it is the only way we can leave our hate behind and move on. Hate is like a weight that keeps you from moving forward. You don't need it, so just leave it behind.

In order to really forgive someone, you must first accept that we are all works in progress. All of us are learning by living. Not everybody learns at the same rate. Furthermore, some people are more sensitive than others. What seems normal for one person may seem offensive or even painful to another. Many of the situations that cause us pain or discomfort originate from these differences. If you were to confront some of the people who hurt you in the past, it's possible that they won't even remember you or having caused you any pain. Probably what they did was not intentional. Probably they would behave differently if the same situation happened today. Do not linger on the mistakes of the past. Move on and keep progressing because I can assure you that you have hurt a lot of people and you don't even know it. It may not have been your fault; it's all about the way we perceive things differently. Even if a person actually intended to hurt another, that person must learn to forgive his or her mistakes. All of us have made mistakes in the past. The best we can do is learn from those mistakes so we don't repeat them.

The same criteria we discussed previously can be used as well to decide the kinds of thoughts that we should allow into our minds. We have to try to make all of our thoughts expressions of truth, beauty, and goodness. A mind filled only with this kind of thinking can be fully utilized the way it was meant to be. A mind with these kinds of thoughts is a clean and attentive mind. The mind is more likely to perceive those things that are similar and familiar. If all your thoughts are similar, if your mind is expressing truth, beauty, and goodness, these are the thoughts your mind will perceive.

The main purpose of the mind is to assist us in creating our reality. We are actually co-creators with the main energy of the universe, our Father. Together we are fabricating our reality and expressing what we first conceive in our minds. Everything we see in our world today was an idea in somebody's mind before it was something we could touch or use. Clear your mind of everything that is useless and leave some space for the inspiration and the opportunities that you are missing because you are not paying attention.

Lastly, you must also learn to control your body. This is what you use to move in the material world. It is your vehicle, your material representation, and the tool you can use to interact in the world. Our bodies have been designed to function almost perfectly with little maintenance. However, many of us have lost connection with our bodies. We also fail to realize the impact that our thoughts have over our health and well-being.

Our thoughts affect our physical bodies. Whenever we succumb to worries and concerns, our bodies suffer. Our bodies release hormones and behave as though we are facing a real threat. These chemical substances are important in the face of danger, but when these chemicals are produced in excess, they alter the proper function of our bodies.

The body responds to the mind's commands. Think about your favorite food. Imagine you are eating it right now. Imagine you have a big plate of it in front of you. Notice that only by imagining this (or simply by reading these words) you can almost taste the food. Your salivary glands start to secrete saliva as if you were actually eating. But this was just a thought. Your body cannot distinguish between what is real and what exists only in your mind; the body just responds to the commands of the mind. It should be obvious then, that well-being actually begins with our mind. The nature of our thoughts determines our health. Many studies have shown that people who consider themselves happier are healthier than others who believe they are unhappy.[2] Optimism and positive thinking have been found to reduce the risks of contracting diseases. In people with cardiovascular disease, the risk of having a cardiovascular event is reduced in optimistic people. Even longevity and frailty are affected by what we think. People who practice positive thinking live longer and stronger than people who are not positive. This is regardless of age, body composition, weight, and diet.

Today we encounter many diseases because we have moved away from our natural habits. We eat too much unnatural food, we sleep too

2 Martin E. P. Seligman, "Positive Health." *Applied Psychology: An International Review* 57 (2008): 3–18.

little, and we don't move enough. Most of us also breathe insufficiently. All this contributes to many of the health problems we face in today's society. To maintain our physical health, we don't need complicated diets, strict exercise programs, or surgical adjustments. We just need to go back to our natural behaviors. First, we must provide our bodies with the nutrients they require. This means we should eat natural, living foods. Most of the food you eat should be something you would find in nature. Vegetables and fruits can be found in nature. You can pick fruit from a tree and eat it on the spot. You can pick vegetables from the ground and eat them without additional preparation. These are natural foods and they are excellent for our bodies. Meats are also natural foods because they come from animals, which we can also find in nature. The further away a particular food is from nature, the less nutrition it provides. If you return to a more natural diet, you will notice how light and good you'll start to feel. Also your mental clarity will greatly improve. Drugs, alcohol, and other chemical substances are not good for our bodies. Furthermore, these substances also damage our brains. You can clearly see that many of these substances are not found in nature. Therefore, these things should never enter your body.

Just by following a natural diet, you will be as healthy as you can be. However, exercise also plays an important role in your well-being. This is another good thing that has been distorted by our society. Sometimes we focus in attaining a "perfect figure," which is determined arbitrarily by the media. We were not all meant to look the same. If you follow a natural diet, your body will adapt to its ideal shape. This does not mean that all of us will look like fashion models—it means that we can be as healthy as possible. Exercise is just a complement to our well-being. In the early part of our history, humans used to walk, hunt, climb, run, lift things, and simply play. In our world today, we no longer need to do any of these things so we need to artificially incorporate exercise into our lives.

The key to exercise is balance. Too little exercise makes our bodies weak and too much exercise has adverse consequences on our health as well. You just need to incorporate activities in your daily life that match some of the activities we used to do in our natural environment. Take walks, play with your children or friends, pick up the laundry, do some chores, take the stairs instead of the elevator. Incorporating this kind of exercise into your life would be more than enough. Now, if your idea of success is competing in the Olympic Games, you will need to do much more. Just be aware that exercise should never be used as a fix for the damages caused by a poor diet. If you eat unnatural food, you will get sick and incur many health risks, even if you run ten miles a day. On the other hand, if your diet is mostly natural, you will be very healthy, even if you exercise only once a week.

We should also consider the external appearance of our bodies. After all, our bodies are our impression to others. Keeping good hygiene is enough. Dress in a way that feels comfortable and show respect for the rules of different cultural groups or organizations. In an ideal world, we should not be forced to dress the same way. Our appearance—our clothes, our hair, and more—should be unique to each individual. However, in our world a lot of people judge others by the way they look, or the way they dress. If you must go to a place where there is a dress code, by all means respect it. There is no point in antagonizing others with something as trivial as clothing. To find success, you must thrive by building relationships with others, not by antagonizing them.

There is something that you should always wear everywhere you go: a smile. People often feel more attracted to people who seem to be happy and approachable. If you are at a party, would you go talk to people who look like they want to fight you? Or would you approach someone who is smiling? A smile shows that you are interested in making friends. Reinforce that smile with a sincere wish to get to know your brothers and sisters in this world, and you will have one of the key elements of success: the ability to relate to everybody.

Becoming the master of yourself is a process. It is not something you will achieve in a short period of time. It is a discipline and requires consistency. If you focus day after day on improving the control you exert over your mind and body, you will begin to find success. Furthermore, you will become a more valuable member of humanity.

People who are successful at what they do and have a passion for their work, project confidence and honesty. Highly successful people have achieved their goals with discipline and work ethics. Otherwise, they would have not made it that far. You know that when such people are assigned a task they will perform it to the best of their ability. Today we need people that can be trusted in such a way, to face the many challenges and problems we see throughout the world.

3

Communicate

All successful people have one thing in common: they didn't do it all by themselves. They didn't do it alone. Communication is the third skill you need to master in order to achieve real and satisfying success. The most successful people are great communicators. They have the ability to communicate their ideas and their desired results so that others understand them. They can literally take an idea and put it into the hands of others who can do something good with it. This is a skill that all people with a high level of success possess, regardless of background, culture, and education. Those who communicate efficiently have a better chance of success than those who don't.

If you really want to be successful, you will have to get help. The truth is that we depend on each other for everything we do in our lives. The idea that a person can do things that won't affect others is just a fallacy. You know by now that even something as personal as the way we think has an impact on others. Everything one person does affects all of us. This is why it's so important to consider carefully the consequences of your actions. Do they meet the criteria of truth, beauty, and goodness? When we act in such a way, only good things will come from our efforts and whatever influence we have on the people around us will be positive.

People are positive by nature. We all want good things. We know that bad things feel bad; we don't like bad. If you or your work provides a benefit to others, they will want that benefit. They will want you to succeed. For example, consider movies. Movies are a lot of work. A lot of people work together to make a movie: from the moment of inspiration to the moment the movie's playing in theaters. When you go to the movie theater, you really don't care about all that. You probably don't know any of the people involved in the production of that movie; you couldn't care less about their lives. They are not your family or friends. However, when you pay money to watch that movie, you want the people who made it to be successful. You are going to the theater to have a good time. You want to relax and forget about the real world for a while. You want the movie to be good. You don't want to spend money and ninety minutes of your time in agony.

Now, if the movie really delivers what you were looking for, you will be satisfied. In fact, you will even tell your friends about the movie and provide free promotion on behalf of people you've never met. You are actually doing some work to make that movie successful. When people find something good, they like to share it.

When you want something to be a success, make sure that it benefits somebody; make sure you are doing something good for someone. This way success is almost impossible to avoid. You will be producing something that is needed, and if you satisfy that need, people will want more and will even recommend you or your service to others. In order to make this happen, you have to change your focus. Instead of thinking about what you can do to be successful, you should be thinking about what you can provide to others. Other ways to formulate this question are: how can I help people? How can I solve this particular problem? What do people want? If you find a satisfactory answer to any of these questions, you will find something that will become very successful. This is the meaning of helping each other. We don't do this because it's the right thing to do. We don't do this because we are trying to be good. We do it because it makes sense.

It's obvious that if we want to progress, to move forward and evolve, we need to work together.

As a result of your life experience and what you've read in this book, you may already have several ideas of things you could do. However, unless you express these ideas and put them into practice, nothing will happen. Nothing will change unless you move your ideas from your mind into the material world. The first step in doing this is to communicate. You have to share your ideas with others in such a way that they know exactly what you mean.

Communication is more than just speaking. Speaking is just sending out a message. Communication occurs when that message is received and understood. In order to complete the communication, the recipient of the message must tell the sender that the message was understood. This is how we know that we have correctly communicated an idea. Through communication, we take something from our mind and transfer it to someone else's mind.

Regardless of what you want to do in life, you will need help to achieve it. Of course, you only need help if you want to succeed. If you want to make movies, you will need people that go to see them. If you want to write a book, you will need people that want to read it. If you are selling something, you will need customers. At every stage, you will need help.

All of us have different talents. All of us enjoy doing different things. In a world as complex as ours, you won't get very far if you do what's already been done. This is known as reinventing the wheel. If you want to progress, you need to do something extra and you need to start where others have finished. So, instead of creating another wheel, try putting four wheels together with a box on top of them, and now you have a cart. Basically, you're taking something that already existed and using it to achieve something new. In this case, your new idea would have not been possible without the idea of the person who invented the wheel.

In everything you do, you can ask for help. You will find that when you discuss your ideas with others they will be able to offer suggestions and new perspectives. Many times throughout your endeavors you may encounter problems or setbacks. If you ask someone for help who has experience in your particular area, you'll find a solution faster than you would by yourself. Take advantage of the experience of others. This is how human knowledge keeps growing.

You need to get away from the individualistic perspective. The world today is driven by competition. People fight to reach their goals before another person beats them to it. Companies are struggling to put their products out there before somebody else does. Sometimes they do it at the expense of quality. What we are in fact doing is fighting for the resources that should be available to everyone. Our economy is based on the premise that only the strong survive; we're not encouraged to share with anybody. The goal is to get rid of competitors and the winner claims the spoils (or the market).

Is this really beneficial to the economy? Is this really a sustainable model? We saw what happened when financial institutions became more aggressively competitive in the subprime debacle. Financial institutions usually trade loans. You might have a mortgage on your house with a particular bank, but usually the owner of the loan changes and you will find that you are paying to different people as time goes by. This is normal and financial institutions get a profit by doing this. Since not everybody can get a loan, mortgage lenders came up with the idea of "subprime" loans. These are higher risk loans that were given to people who would have not qualified to get a regular loan. Financial institutions saw that there was a big market for this kind of loans and aggressively started to promote and offer this new service. They started competing among each other and became more and more flexible in their loan requirements, trying to get the most of the market.

Apparently they forgot that there was a reason why some people are not approved for regular loans. Most of the people with subprime loans found that they could not meet the conditions of their loans and could not pay. Suddenly a lot of people were defaulting on their mortgages and a lot of houses were repossessed. Financial institutions started to sell their subprime loans and general panic ensued. Housing values plummeted, lots of financial institutions went bankrupt, and a global financial crisis ensued.

Ethical collaboration is a more sustainable model than competition. By ethical collaboration, I mean the free exchange of ideas and expertise in order to create the best products/services possible using shared resources. Financial institutions could have decided to get together and plan how to take advantage of the subprime market. They could have distributed their subprime loans according to the size of individual institutions. They would have been sharing the market, not fighting for it. At the end, even if that market turned out to be unprofitable, they would have shared the loss too. No financial institutions would have closed, the confidence of the public in the financial sector would have not diminished, and the impact of the problem would have been greatly minimized.

Get away from the competitive frame of mind. The world is big enough for all of us and you don't really need to fight for your piece of success. Success is only limited by our ideas and by the way we face our world. There are not really natural limits to success. Whatever you do, share your ideas. You'll see that your ideas, with the help of others, will become more clear and powerful. But to do this you need to communicate efficiently.

There are many ways to learn about communication and many organizations dedicated to teaching you this. Toastmasters is one of the most inexpensive and effective of such organizations because it teaches you by giving you practical experience. Search for the help of experts on communication (or any other topic), and you will save a great deal of time and effort. Communication is not really that hard, but it requires practice. The key is to focus on the message you want to convey. Understand that when you are trying to express your ideas, others may not understand them at first. Others will not necessarily have your background or experience. Whenever you are trying to make others understand your ideas, be willing to listen to their questions and objections. It is there where the real opportunity of being understood lies. Assume that when nobody asks questions it's because you did not explain your idea correctly. If your idea is a good one and it is understood, people will want to know more. Remember that people want more of good things. If you show them something that will benefit them, they will want it.

When you focus on the message, you tend to do everything you can to make sure the other party understands what you are trying to say. Focusing your attention and efforts on the message makes you appear more authentic. If you focus on the benefit you expect to obtain from your idea, others will perceive that. If you are worried about rejection or the judgment of others, you will quit at the first chance. When you are focused on actually making others understand what you really mean, you will transport them to your world by any means necessary. You will use all the resources available to you. You will use speech, gestures, and visual aids.

The most successful salesmen are not the ones who describe all the features of their products. The ones who make the sale are those who show how the product will provide a benefit for the potential buyer. They will show how the product can be used to solve a problem for the customer. People will know when they are offered something that will help them achieve their goals, and they will want it.

In order to show the value of an idea, you need to show the results. If you have an idea that will provide some benefit to others, be clear about what the benefit is. For example, if you want to start a literacy program for uneducated children in third world countries, you could say something like this: "We need to help our children to discover the wonderful things they could learn if they could read." This is poetic, pretty, and sweet. However, it will not take you anywhere. "What's the point?" someone may ask. A more effective description could be: "Having a high number of uneducated people costs the government X dollars. If we teach children how to read, they are more likely to get an education and we will save X dollars." This is simple and shows how your idea really helps people. By emphasizing your desired outcome, you will move people toward action. Be visionary with ideas and be practical with results.

At the most basic level, in order to share your ideas efficiently, you must: focus on the message, make sure they understand what you mean, and show the results. It is possible, however, that when you share an idea, people may raise some valid objections. Pay attention to these objections and accept them when they are real. Take some time to really consider the validity of your idea in light of this new information. If an idea is good, it will prevail in the face of objections and disbelief. In fact, objections are a good way to evaluate ideas. Also, you will gain more evidence of the validity of an idea if the objections can be overcome. You will notice that in the process of sharing your ideas they will become more refined and you will be able to express them better. Great ideas are not thought once. They were conceived by someone, they were shared, they were modified to be more effective, and, finally, they are implemented.

Your ideas are perhaps your must valuable resource in finding success. However, if you don't share your ideas, they are useless. Learn to communicate efficiently and learn to share what's on your mind. You already have great ideas inside you. You have solutions for problems that others have never imagined. Don't let your ideas be wasted. Share them.

4

Find Your Passion

Don't you ever wonder why some people seem to find success so easily? Why is it so hard for others? All your life you have been taught that in order to be successful you have to work hard. However, this is not exactly true. In fact, if you are working hard for something, you are not going to be successful.

One of the main attributes of success is doing what you love and becoming the best you can be at it. When you are doing what you love, it shouldn't feel like work. It should be a joy. It should be fun. Those who have fun doing what they like are more likely to be successful. When you do what you enjoy, you are living in the present. There is no other place you would rather be. There is nothing else you would prefer to do. You are entirely focused. You are in the zone. These are all qualities required to find success within a particular profession or activity. On the other hand, if your work feels like a chore, if you feel like you are working hard, or if you can't wait to go home from your job, then you'll never achieve excellence. You'll never be the best you can be.

You need to explore and see what you would like to do. When considering your options, think about what you would enjoy doing day after day, for the rest of your life. In order to do this, you have to clarify your idea of success. Success is a general concept. It does not deal with specific elements like money, status, or fame. A good definition of success does not include results. You are successful when you are doing what you most enjoy, regardless of the expected result. Success is just a consequence of your passion. Understand that when you are really good at something, success will come easily. Being successful will inevitably provide results, but your efforts should be focused on the process.

In order to achieve success, you must be doing something you are passionate about. You will be having fun even when others may call what you do work. When you enjoy what you do, you can keep doing the same thing over and over again. Every day you are excited to start doing it. Your creativity is at its highest. You are coming up with new ideas constantly and you can't wait to try them. When obstacles or problems arise, you face them with enthusiasm and enjoy the challenges. You are learning constantly and you're getting better all the time.

At this point, others will start noticing your increasing levels of expertise and excellence. You will begin to stand out and start drawing attention. The things, products, or services you provide will be better each time. Therefore, more and more people will want to consume what you offer. This is when you will begin to see results. Additional results will come, while you are doing something you enjoy immensely. You will be in a circle of increasing productivity. Your efforts are motivated by your passion, your love for what you do, and the good results you achieve. These results will include the satisfaction of your basic needs, like financial independence, quality of life, time for family, and others. You can have everything you need; you really can. Remove from your mind the idea that you don't deserve it. You do. You'll be doing something good for others. You'll be doing something that benefits people. It's fair to expect compensation for your efforts, even if you don't feel like you're actually working.

You may already have some sense of where your passion lies. When you choose the activity you want to focus on, you just need to consider two things. First, it must be something you enjoy. You have only one life. Why would you want to spend it doing something you don't enjoy? Second, your activity should produce something that is beneficial to somebody else. Use the truth, beauty, and goodness criteria. Are you helping somebody? Are you making a task easier? Are you providing information or instruction? Are you providing solutions? The list of things that match these criteria is endless, but if you don't deliver something that people want, you will not be successful. You can have a lot of fun doing what you want to do, but you will still need to do something else to live. You need to make a good living doing what you love.

When we think of success, we usually think about money. This is the wrong place to start. Money in and of itself does not mean success. There are lots of people with a lot of money who are miserable. Some people focus all their efforts on accumulating money, yet once they have it, they still don't feel as if they've accomplished anything. They either keep working blindly, or they end up confused, thinking that life makes no sense at all. This happens because they focused on the result, the money, and not on the process.

It's not that money is bad. You need it. You should have as much as you need to ensure your quality of life and even your pleasures. But money is just one result of doing what you love. It's not the only component of success. In fact, one day money will not be necessary anymore. Money is just a representation of what we possess. When we give money in exchange for something else we are just bartering. We are so out of touch with our spirituality that we cannot think about giving away something without getting something else in return. Similarly, it is hard for us to think that we will be getting something without a cost involved.

However, this has not always been the case. During our early days as humans in nature, we shared food and shelter freely. If one member of the tribe found a source for food, the others were notified to get what they needed. Only recently in our history have people been unable to obtain food without paying a price. How did things get so bad? I'm not proposing that we go back to live in caves, but we have lost that sense of being a group, of caring about our neighbors. As we keep evolving and progressing, more people will realize that work is not just a way to avoid hunger. It is another form of self-expression and realization. People will work for pleasure and will offer their products or services as an artist offers his or her work: to do something good for others and self. We will not have to worry about satisfying our needs. Some day our needs will be met by those who love to provide the things we need. If one person needs to eat, another person who loves to cook will provide the food. If the person who cooks needs clothes, someone else who loves to make clothes will provide the best quality products. We will live in a world where we can simply go somewhere and get what we need without any effort. We'll be working at the top of our game, providing the best products and services in history because everyone will be doing what they love most. In this world, success will become more real, truer. It will not be about simply satisfying a need, since all our needs will be satisfied from birth. Success will mean doing something that we enjoy in order to contribute to our world and to keep growing spiritually.

But we are not there yet, and in the meantime, we need to cover our most basic needs. You can do this by finding your passion. We are at a point in our evolution where we should start to look for those things that make us better and help us grow. Early in our development as humans we needed to survive and do whatever was necessary. Now we need to focus on living, not just surviving.

The utopia I mentioned above is not only possible, it will be the result of the efforts we are all making. When you are successful, you are contributing a little bit toward a better future for our world. You have a debt to all those who came before you because they prepared the world and made it what it is now. It's true that there are still many problems that need solutions, but we are not living in caves anymore, at least most of us aren't. The best way to honor this debt to our ancestors is by leaving the world a better place than we found it.

You also have a responsibility to those who will come after you: your descendants, your children and their children. As your decisions shape your life and your future, our collective decisions will shape the future of our world. If we all focus on providing what this world needs, if we do what we love and this results in something that contributes a little bit to make things better, we are fulfilling our responsibility to the future. You can elevate the importance of whatever you do by realizing that you are contributing to your world and you are shaping a better future.

Think about this. Many people will be reading this book because they bought in on the Internet. You will obtain great benefits from this book and your success will contribute to improve the lives of countless others. But you could only buy this book on the Internet because somebody once had the idea of making computers communicate with each other. In turn, that idea would have not been possible without computers. Computers are possible because somebody thought it would be nice to have machines that could be programmed to do different things. But this was not possible without transistors and electronic components. These could only be conceived because somebody discovered electricity. Can you see how something as simple as getting a book has required the effort of a chain of people throughout history? For that matter, it would not be possible for you to read these words without first learning to read, so be thankful to your first grade teacher as well. We are all connected. We are part of a whole and everything we do influences others—today and tomorrow.

When you decide to be successful, it's not just you who will achieve success. You are actually making things better for many others around you, even those who will come after you. You may be thinking that your decision is a selfish one. This is not the case. Deciding to be successful is a decision that means you will not be one more problem in this world. You will be taking care of yourself, and you will be helping others with the products and services you provide—the results of doing what you love. Humanity wants you to be successful; all of us need you to be successful. Our Father expects you to be successful. It is a win-win situation. Nothing good comes when somebody fails. Remember, we all want what is good for us. You have to be successful and you have to help others do the same.

By the time we select what we want to do for the rest of our lives, how many ways of earning a living do we know? We usually know about a dozen of possible careers from which we can choose. However, there are hundreds, even thousands of ways to make a living in this world. In fact, there should be one way for each one of us, currently about seven billion. All of us should not be doing the same thing, the same way.

All of us have our comfort zones. This is the sum of what we know and accept. Our comfort zones also reflect the ideas we have about ourselves. We don't like to venture into the unknown. We don't like to be in a place where we don't know what to expect. Exploring is just that. It is moving away from what we know in order to see what else is out there. Sometimes, it even involves facing our fears and anxieties.

Your mind is limited by the things you think you know. When I was growing up, I believed that the best way to make a good living was to become an engineer, and so I did. This is what I did. But there are millions of people in this world who are not engineers and who are successful people. My choices were very limited, but I was lucky to find something that I enjoyed and was good at. Some of my friends had the same notion about engineering being the only way. They were not as lucky; they turned out not to be very good at it, so they just quit.

My friends didn't need counseling or vocational information. They just needed to change their perspective of what was important. They moved from what they didn't like, but instead of searching for what they liked, they succumbed to survival mode. They just did the first thing they could easily find to make ends meet. This is fine for a little while, but real success will come only if you find your passion.

Many of them went on to find the first job available to them, and they settled there. They would have fared a lot better if they had had more alternatives to choose from. It's not that they didn't work hard.

They did, but they didn't like what they were doing, so at the first opportunity they got away. And this, by the way, is the best thing you can do if you are doing something today that you don't enjoy. Your time is yours to live the way you want. Don't waste it.

In my case, I came from a science background. I am an engineer and enjoy mathematics and logical problems. I deal with concrete and practical issues. This is what I have been doing for most of my life. Now, after a time of exploration, I have found that I enjoy writing. I remember taking literature classes in school and hating them. I remember how much easier it was for me to solve math problems than to write essays. After I finished school, I didn't want to write anymore.

However, after a couple of years I started writing little things. Little by little, I started to like it. Now, I can see myself making a living doing this. I enjoy exploring my ideas through writing and I had no formal training to do it. I don't consider myself a good writer. What I write is edited and revised by professionals who enjoy the more technical aspects of writing. However, I love doing it and the ideas are still mine, even after someone else has helped me to articulate them better. But I would not be doing this if I had not explored, if I had not stepped out from what I thought I knew about myself. I had to leave my comfort zone. I had to experience a little discomfort before I discovered this new way of expressing myself.

You can only achieve success doing what you love. Even if you make a lot of money and satisfy all your needs, it won't feel like success if you do something you don't enjoy. Finding what you love, finding your passion, is the only way you will become the best you can be. If you love something, you will keep doing it over and over again, until you master it. If you have a passion, little problems, obstacles, and adversity will never discourage you. Success doesn't have to be hard. You can easily find success at anything, but only if you have a passion for it.

5

Success!

You now know all you need to do in order to find success, *your* success. You can achieve your goals and make your dreams a reality if you align your life and your will with the energy of the universe, with what I call the Father's will. You may put any name to this main universal energy that you like. Some call it the universe, some call it Love, and some call it God. I prefer Father because it indicates that we are dealing with a person. It also represents a personal relationship with Him and provides an indication of the intentions that He has for each of us. You are a beloved son of this Father, and being the most perfect father you can imagine, He wants the best for you. Search for your Father, and you will be given the wisdom that will help you triumph.

If you make the effort to understand and use the four principles explained in this book, you will be successful. In fact, success will come easily. Decide, master yourself, communicate, and find your passion. Notice that this is the recipe for a journey of exploration, in which the main goal is to find yourself and the connection you have with the origin of all things—the Father. The four principles of success may be described as opening yourself to Love, letting it work in you, sharing it, and letting it flow to others through you. This is a process in which each step will lead to the next one, but all steps can be practiced at the same time.

I wrote this book because I have seen so many people struggling to find success and not getting anywhere. I believe that this happens for two main reasons: not knowing what you love to do and having unrealistic expectations. It is very important that you dedicate your efforts to an activity that you truly enjoy. Make sure to take the time to find out what you would love to be doing for a living. If you do this your work will be your pleasure. Success usually doesn't just happen by chance. However, most people make finding success harder than it has to be. There is work involved, but if you work in something you like you will never feel like you are working hard. Find what you would like to do even if you were not being paid to do it. This is what will make you successful.

The second factor that prevents people from finding success is to have unrealistic expectations. If your idea of success is to be very famous and the richest person on Earth, you might have a hard time achieving your dreams. Not everybody can be famous and not everybody can have millions of dollars. The truth is that not everybody needs that to be happy and to live a fulfilling life.

Keep in mind that balance is the key to making success sustainable. Even if you love immensely what you do, you can get tired of it if you don't balance what you do with the other aspects of your life. Allow some time for friends, family, and relationships. Also leave some time for learning and more exploration. Always keep growing. Always keep moving. You will find that you can be successful at more than one thing. It is okay to find and try new things and discover new areas through which you can grow. There can be many things that spark your passion. Your life should be full of exploration, learning, and, of course, fun. There are some basic lessons we all need to learn, such as how to live in harmony with others and how to use our intellects and our resources in such a way that we all enjoy life and keep progressing. Remember your responsibility to your brothers and sisters in this world. You know how to be successful and you will remember what you did once you have found your success. Share your knowledge. Help others enjoy the same things you do. Helping others to find their success is beneficial for all.

Money will come with success. You need it. Use it well, but don't love it. Money is just a means to satisfy your needs. At some point, you will have to decide how much is enough. There's only so much you need. In fact, all your needs and pleasures can be met with less money than you think. When you have more than you need, don't fall into the trap of accumulation. You need to save money for you, for the years when you cannot work anymore, and for your family. Don't keep more than you need because money that is not being used is just nothing. Unused money is like a good idea that you never share. It does nothing and it helps nobody. When you reach the point of having more money than you need, do something good with it. There are many problems in our world, and you can help to solve at least one of these problems. You could also use your money to support somebody else who is trying to solve a problem. Don't buy more toys if you're not going to play with them. Don't fill your life with clutter. You will know when you reach the saturation point. After this, whatever you do with your money is up to you. Be smart about it and remember that what you do will affect all of us.

Success is not a final state you reach. It is a process. Success is what you feel when you are doing something that you love, when you feel that what you do will help somebody else. Money, recognition, and other benefits are only the result of doing what you love with passion. Success is a consequence of your passion. You can feel successful even when the results are not there yet. Don't worry, they will come, and very soon, sooner than you think. But if you reach a point where you're seeing good results without enjoying what you're doing, it's time to move on. Maybe during this process you will find that what helped you get to one level is not going to help you move forward to the next level. When this happens, change accordingly. You may have been doing something you loved for many years, but now the satisfaction is gone. It's time to find something else. Keep looking for ways to grow. Keep exploring. Most of the things we do are just stepping-stones on our way to becoming better. Never let the past get in the way of the future. Live always in the present and build your future one day at a time.

All you need to be successful is here. The title of this book refers to the fact that by applying the principles you read about here, you will find success. The title also serves to remind you that right here, right now, you already have everything you need to be successful. You have always had it, and nobody can take it away from you. It is your divine right to find the way to get the most from your life, and to grow to be the best you can be.